Wilma had a lot of drawings. They
were all pictures of girls.

"I like drawing clothes," Wilma said.
Biff looked at Wilma's pictures.
"They are good," she said.

Chip was painting a picture. He was
painting a volcano.

Wilma moved her leg. She kicked
Chip's water over.
"Whoops!" said Wilma. "Sorry."

The water ran over Chip's picture.
Chip was cross.
"My picture is a mess now!" he said.

Chip flicked paint over Wilma's picture.
"Your drawings are silly," he said.
Biff told Chip to say sorry.

Chip was too cross to say sorry. He flicked paint at Wilma. Then the key began to glow.

The magic took them to a volcano. It
looked like Chip's painting. But where
was Chip?

"Look at those girls," gasped Wilma.
"They look like the ones in my
drawings. Look at their clothes."

The girls called to Wilma.
"Do you like my top?" said a girl. "Do you like my boots?"

Suddenly, the volcano began to spit out blobs of red paint. Splat! A big blob landed by Biff.

"Come on! Run!" yelled Biff. "Run! Or
the volcano will get us."
"I can't run in these boots," said a girl.

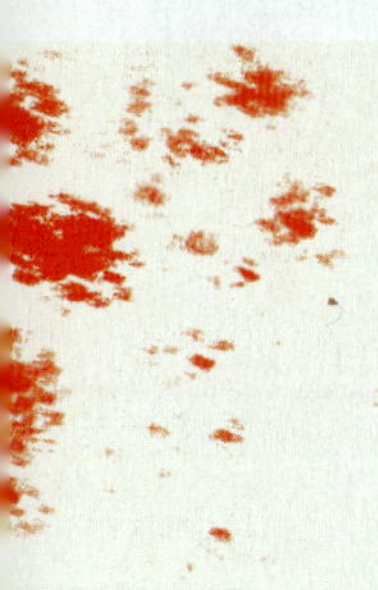

"Run!" yelled Wilma.
"We can't," said a girl. "I can't run in this dress!"

Splat! Red blobs landed everywhere.
"It's red paint!" said Biff.
Splat! A red blob hit a girl.

Red paint began to gush out of the volcano. It looked like a big, red river.

Wilma had an idea. She began to
draw jeans and tops. Biff helped her.

"Quick! Put these on," said Wilma.
"Oh! We like these," said the girls.

"Now run!" called Wilma.
They all ran.

Chip was in the paint river.
"Help! Help!" he called. "Get me out!"

Biff and Wilma saw Chip.
"Stop!" they called. "We must get
him out."

Wilma had an idea. She drew a long
rope.
"Hold on, Chip," she called.

They pulled Chip out.
"I'm glad this is only paint and not a
real volcano," said Biff.

"Phew!" said Chip. "Am I glad you
pulled me out!"
The magic key began to glow.

"Now are you sorry, Chip?" said Biff.
Chip had a blob of paint on him.
"I am," he said. "Sorry!"